CRUISE THROUGH LOVE

A PERSONAL STORY

SOHINI DUTT

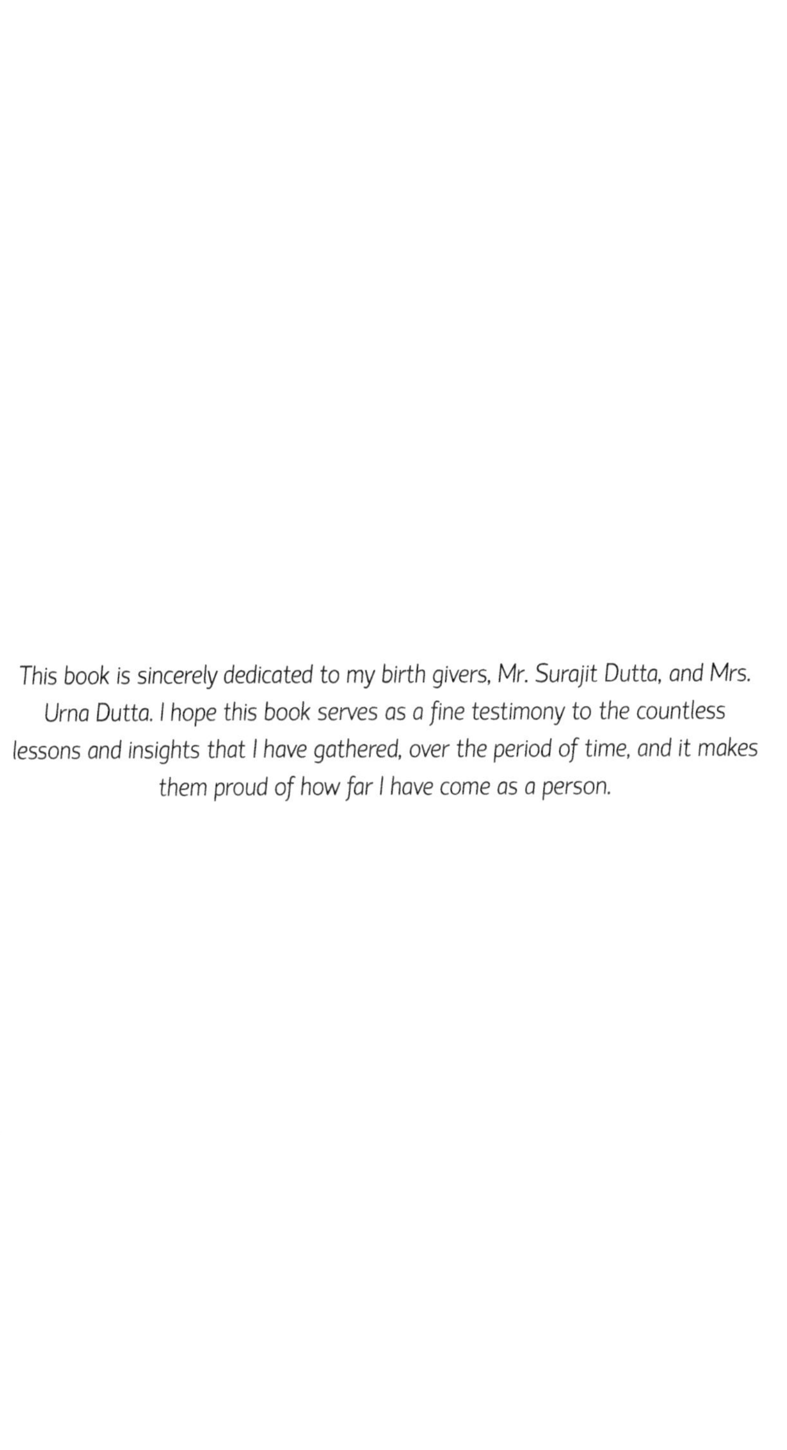

This book is sincerely dedicated to my birth givers, Mr. Surajit Dutta, and Mrs. Urna Dutta. I hope this book serves as a fine testimony to the countless lessons and insights that I have gathered, over the period of time, and it makes them proud of how far I have come as a person.

Contents

Contents

Preface

Growing up as the eldest daughter in a nuclear brown family, comprising of working parents, it is inevitable to turn out as a reticent and introverted woman, who takes pleasure in steering clear from other individuals. I had a close-knit circle of barely two friends (and I still do), and the rest were all acquaintances who happened to share the class with me. As would be conventionally expected, I too grew up to confine my childhood solely to academics, and spent most of my younger days taking good care of my brother. My fairly decent scores served as significant points of validation, that made me feel I was worthy of getting my parents' attention. Typically deprived of their precious time, and regard, I began to look for similar heed from men who confessed their fondness for me. More than drawing on their characteristics that would describe them as potential lovers, I rather looked for someone who would just sit beside me and listen to what I had to say, a person who would ask me about my day and specifically enquire about the best and worst, because he would be interested in knowing it all. So you could clearly say as a young teenager, I was oblivious of what love meant as an idea. Rather, the slightest attention from a stranger across the busy street would make me feel wanted, and I'd develop a sudden infatuation if it's coupled with an attractive personality. Such a process more or less defines my initial experiences with love and relationships, and needless to mention, the inevitable heartbreaks, since the love was never real.

Fast forward to the time when my personal experiences in this regard had become significant enough to shape me as a mentally disturbed young woman in her early twenties, who refuses to trust easy, and spends her nights over thinking until three in the morning, about how one sunny day she might be deceived again, and just like that, history would repeat itself. Needless to mention, my failed friendships added on to the misery, and one fine day, I did find myself all alone, scrolling through countless messages, deeply wondering what went wrong. And then the answer knocked on my brain, and I reckoned love for the self was what was needed for my scores to go back up, and for my friends to accept me as a normal human being, rather than a kid with a disturbing childhood.

This book bears sheer testimony to all such experiences of mine, and (hopefully) scrupulously highlights the journey and growth, from a phase of misery and hopelessness, to a phase of reckoning, and maturity- a steady but worthwhile realization of the need for loving the self, before giving it all to a stranger who has just been a day's friend.

Even though affection is bound to develop more than once, knowing one's worth is of supreme importance before placing the supposed Prince Charming on the pedestal again. That's life, that's the mantra to the 'cruise through love'.

Acknowledgements

As an unfortunate but considerably significant consequence of the consistent blows that were hurled at me, throughout my past encounters with men, I had fallen victim to moments of sheer hopelessness, and overwhelmed with soaring pessimistic thoughts. It was around this time, that fate brought me closer to some individuals (who continue to have an ascendancy in my life), who knowingly surpassed every barrier to ensure I was in safe hands, and my mind was at peace.

The first person I owe every reckoning to is Rahul Chaudhary. I would like to extend my heartfelt gratitude and thanks to his consistent efforts into making me into whatever I am today. The slightest of what I have learnt about happiness and the art of 'letting go', is all a result of our parked car conversations, real life experiences, and teaching by example. Less of a friend and more of a brother, he has been the one strong pillar who has stood by me, even after witnessing me zero down with time.

Words would fall short to express my gratitude for having crossed paths with Alkeshwr Singha, who has come as a blessing in disguise to me. Even when he watched me cross all limits to sanity, he chose to hang on still, and give me life lessons that someday would start making sense to me. He has been a refined man, in terms of character, reckoning, and maturity, so much so that his insights about life have made me into a woman who now chooses to smile, rather than shed a tear, when life throws lemons at her.

Sincere thanks to my roommate back in New Delhi, Shatakshi Juyal, who has always been there to make me understand the inevitable consequences of life, and how one could do nothing but nod in acceptance, with a smile on their face. It is from her that I've learnt how "people leaving and choosing not to stay" is inevitably a part of life.

Heartfelt thanks to my college mate, and close friend, Trupti Gehlot, who was always at the beck and call, and never shied away from going beyond what was needed. I feel blessed to have been gifted with her company, and affection, for such friendships are to be treasured, in today's time.

My old school friend, Sharang Goswami, who fortunately shifted to Delhi for work purposes, made sure to give me company whenever I was in need of some. He would travel for an hour and come all the way from Noida, to just sit and talk, so I'd not think about the deepest end of the story, and rather shift my attention to the brighter side.

Last but not the least; I owe a lot to my parents, Mr. Surajit Dutta, and Mrs. Urna Dutta, who have persistently guided me through every ordeal of life, and taught me to never give up, no matter how difficult and arduous the journey of life gets. Patience and sincerity is what I've learnt from them, and what has shaped me as a level-headed human.

Flow Of Events

The layout of the book is such that it attempts to meticulously portray the steady transition from a phase of heartbreak, resulting from immense trust, and diminished self love, so much so that it fools the lover into believing the love is nothing but an expression of obsession and madness; to a phase of self-growth and reckoning, in which realization strikes that early attachments are an inevitable peril of young love.

Chapter 1-11 delineates the kind of love that had been existing between two young lovers, prior to the summoning of its unannounced end. They talk of the tiny, little moments of togetherness, and memories that had a story to tell.

Chapter 12-16 express the grief and misery resulting from the sudden culmination of something so intimate. They seek to highlight the failed coping mechanisms, moments of sheer helplessness, and the inability to deal with the reality that now looks so evil, and eats on the soul.

Chapter 17-22 show the birth of something new yet again, after a short pause of two months. There are signs of clear affection, promises, and acceptance, but time is what shall decide the fate of this new intimacy. It could be the start of a kind of love that would consume us entirely, or it could just be the Lord's wish to reassure that good still exists.

The final segment of the book, "Reckonings of the past", is a straightforward note to the past, complete with realizations and corrections, accepting the conflicted reality in which love wasn't really what it seemed like.

CHAPTER ONE

A fresh start

I would like to think of life as a spectacular novel consisting of at least a million different chapters,
Chapters that represent a plethora of possibilities, choices, and situations, and as they call it, you are "the main character", simply changing roles in every succeeding story.
To my spent soul, some chapters did come to appear as apocalyptic- sections in which I barely pulled through, to tell the world I survived.
And then there were other chapters which stunned me in disbelief, I found myself baffled as and when I came to acknowledge transitions and impermanence as a constant part of life.
Even though my terribly bruised yet throbbing heart didn't shy away from loving again, and my scorched but eager soul did not resist new friendships, nothing changed the truth- the undeniable truth that people leave, sooner or later.
In this ever-changing and fast-pacing world that is impregnated with drama, adrenaline, and excitement I realize it's only I who can wait to see me grow through it all.
I've been flipping through the chapters ever since my high school years. And it is now that I've finally reached a chapter that I seem to like. This new chapter feels transformative, rejuvenating, exciting, and full of thrill.
It feels like my rough skinned, tanned, tiny little palm, finally fits someone else's way too perfectly.

With all due respect to the past patterns, and the established philosophy of change, I did lose people disguised as friends and loved ones. But this time hopefully, this chapter would culminate into an ever so exciting climax, and I just can't wait to witness what it holds for me.
So if life is a novel, I'm now starting to become a bibliophile. And I'm in love with this transition for now, if not forever.

CHAPTER TWO

The blossoming of something new

If it weren't for the caramel ruffled hair, then it was surely about the uncontrollable laughter that somehow managed to make my eyes crease, as a teardrop would sneak out of each.

I could read that word dancing in your head, as you looked me in the eye and pulled me closer with each step.

The night would grow younger, and the glittered sky would give us company, as nostalgia would grip our souls and remind us of our inception.

Even though I'd be profoundly intoxicated, and my eyes would barely manage to refuse the approaching sleep, I'd know I want you to slowly whisper as my ears feel a slow tickle, "I love you".

I can imagine my favorite artist playing, as I make my cliché moves only to disappoint you with my dance. You'd eventually grab me by the waist, as I rest my head against your well-shaped chest, almost like a baby drifting to sleep in his mother's arms after an eventful day.

I'd giggle once or twice. I admit my drunk self has dozens of inside jokes to recall, as you just stand in front and stare, waiting for me to sober up.

I feel my insides loosen up, as if I'd just let go off a heavy weight. I could breathe easy, as I realize I let go of the damage that had been existing.

I didn't know a power in me existed all this while, the power to let things be and wait for the good to arrive, even after draining myself of optimism and the hope for better days.

You look like art- the picture that I had imagined a decade ago and which finally sprung to life, so much so that I can touch and feel it, I can live it. Dreams do come true, I imagine.

I reckon you're my shadow-self, just in another gender. We think the same, and are the same, but you my dear, are a hardened man, accomplished with consummate elegance.

There's a comfortable silence, as we let our eyes talk. I can see your cheekbones blush a little, as I too catch myself go crimson. All those stories of self-loathing and self-abandonment had finally come to a close, as a new chapter began with a random night at the nightclub.

The crowd cheered and grooved, but we never spoke a word. But that was until we parted in hours, and something seemed out of place- we weren't together.

Sheer gratitude to destiny that led me to your way and tonight I boast of a movie plot that narrates how I became yours to keep.

Maybe it's this newfound passion that gives me chills each time you call my name. Nevertheless of one thing I'm certain, and that is I'm here to see what happens next.

CHAPTER THREE

Hopes and wishes

The night before, I had an unusual dream. It kept my baggy eyes fully aware about how it was just the moon and me, as the night casually drifted past the midnight hour.

It has not been more than fourteen days that I have begun to feel alive once again, happy in this soul and flesh that once made me wince. Yet it feels like I have lived a year already, accepting how the universe had aligned with me.

In that dream, I saw pain. It looked like a disturbing documentary, which had nothing but damage and trauma- the kind that never faded away, but chose to stay, until the will in me was courageous enough to force it out the door.

For a brief moment, I racked my brain for an answer. Why did I have to see it all after all these tiny little moments of pure affection?

Something inside of me urged me to analyze the whole process. And I reckoned how all I needed to do was wait- wait for my story to be true. Time had been my only answer to the plethora of miseries that I held on to.

I had been alive for merely twenty-two years, but all this while I knew my soul was spent and finished. I was drained of life and blood, even though one could claim I smiled. Probably that's the beautiful irony about open wounds that refuse to heal.

I was firm in the belief that this was my reality. I convinced the mind to accept a conflicted present as the normal discourse, and all I needed was to pull through.

It is now that I know the cause of the dream- the realization that time doesn't forget, but discerns. And that cognition corrects your notion of the "real good".
I smile as I see, I am around good. Finally, and hopefully.

CHAPTER FOUR

If all goes well..

An absolute state of turmoil resides outside this room,

A land of rush and heightened emotions, a city screaming with colossal damage,

I see mortals with cold shoulders, and dear faces with distorted minds,

But serenity upon entering here, where your brawny but comforting arms offer me solace,

The furiously beating heart soothes down, as the blood within calms its rush.

What's it in your single touch, I wonder. It's as if you're the diary I had poured my thoughts into, when I was ten.

Your angelic face stares at me, with love so overwhelming. That each time I catch them, my face flushes pink.

There's something about your words, they seem to have solutions for my sorrows. Not the ones we find in books, or the advice that lay men speak of, but reflections that could guide me to the brighter end of the tunnel.

No false alarms, or fancy poetry. Simply life and you as the experienced.

Are you the real one? Or someone who's a lesson? Or do I call you the gift that has been sent down to me?

As I lay my chest in yours, and wrap my body against yours, your slow breaths assure me that pain is slowly dripping down my body.

It was only last month when I pleaded for a few days, to escape this miserable life,

and now that I stayed in, I feel closer to living.

The one thought that however pesters me all day,

Is to wonder if it'll all last forever, just this way?

CHAPTER FIVE

To tame it all

To fall in love is a universal experience. If your stomach twists and turns unusually when you see them, if your heart beat fastens its pace when they look you in the eye, and if you feel your blood rushing furiously as they let out a smile, then you must know it's love that has consumed your senses, as you reckon you're no longer able to push it back. Falling in love is that easy.

What's nightmarish however is whether that someone loves you back; whether they spot the shine in your eyes as your cheeks flush red, whether they catch sight of the momentary crease in your skin extending from both sides of your nose to the corners of the mouth as you struggle to hide the smile, and whether they sense the heightened rush of emotions in you as you get all jittery and begin feeling butterflies inside. And if they do discover it all, and sense a similar desire, then it's nothing but two lovers destined to unite. And love happens just like that- a kind of love that is driven by unfathomable passion, the consistent and overwhelming urge to see each other every day of the week, and the irresistible impulses that drive you bonkers. A love that offers you adventure and makes you step out of the ordinary, is what pushes you to crave for it every passing day. Love intoxicates your soul to the extent that it becomes an arduous challenge to live a day without them.

I had become the fortunate victim of such a love almost three months back, and ever since not a day has passed when I didn't succumb to the cruelties of distance. Surely a favored generation, we need not wait for handwritten letters to arrive, neither do we have to strive for phone calls. However when the ever-increasing farness and the overwhelming burden of assignments keep you within bounds and confines me to limits, then how do I tame that furiously beating heart inside of me that shrieks in agony as it grieves for your absence? How do I teach it to not get nostalgic each time a day of togetherness comes to a close? How do I reason with the foolishly anxious mind of mine that just can't think of anything else but you? How do I convince my longing soul that it must not give up on hope? How do I summon all my strength to force it all into submission, when the soaring emotions in me are just not willing to listen? The day you come up with an answer to it all, I shall finally teach my heart to love in limits.

CHAPTER SIX

The lessons

Sixteen years is undeniably a very long time to speak of, but regardless I fortunately concluded that I could withstand the most tumultuous times, with a smile that was unbelievable, and a demeanor that was flawless. It was as if I was teaching myself to somehow thrive inside a conflicted and brutally damaged soul, while eventually transforming it into a resistant and indestructible self, which at some point I knew I would refuse to believe in. The irony of it all was the interesting fact that I was capable of stopping the monster without turning myself into one. Although I had fallen victim to hatred and cold-hearted sentences expressing themselves through violent actions, I still take pride in saying that empathy and benevolence yet keep me company. I guess those sixteen years weren't just never-ending months of sorrow and unwanted despair, but a genuinely long enough time to mould me into a tougher self that could stay put through everything, even though slowly withering away.

Sixteen years later, I stumble upon a kind of love that makes me believe in the possibility of permanence, and the achievability of absolute happiness. Sixteen years later I'm told by a stranger that I am worthy of a love that consumes me, and I am capable of being loved generously. Even though the shadows of danger were dancing somewhere in the backdrop of it all, a sliver of hope somehow shown in me, and I held his hand firmly, as if allowing myself to accept the idea that I too was deserving of another chance at living. Walking down the memory lane, I did recall the innumerable days when my hope stemmed up from nothing but lighted candles and habitual prayers, all directed to someone who had never paid me a visit when I looked up to the stars and sobbed silently. Even though I knew none but He had heard me, I had never heard him speak a word that would console me. But exactly sixteen years later I reckon, it was only He who watched it all, and waited for my time to come. Maybe all that emotional outpour was necessary for me to embrace supreme bliss when it came to me.

But then again, my insides were still raw. The wounds are still fresh, and the heart still aces at nights when the stars refuse to show. Every truth somehow hints at a lie, even when there couldn't be the slightest possibility. Every act of acceptance feels like a façade that would soon fade away. Every word of assurance sounds like fabricated half-truths. Even when I know this love is the poetic kind that they write in books, how do I refill the empty void that now screams of insecurities and distrust because of what happened over a period of sixteen long years? Even though I had picked myself up and walked through it all to stand here today, how do I confidently claim that I'm yet again ready to fight a new battle, without knowing what awaits me? Someone told me it takes time to gather yourself. What I fear however is what if it takes me longer than how long the other person is willing to wait for?

I have moved past the falsified version of love that tormented me for sixteen long years, and that I am certain of. But how do I lay faith in the sudden version of unconditional love, knowing all I've ever gotten in return is abandonment? The never-ending fear still holds me back each night, but this time I know I'll conquer it. My only reinforcement is time, and I hope this man offers it to me in abundance, for what I fear the most is to be left stranded with a broken heart, only for not being able to gather myself within the said amount of time. no wonder now I know why the world complains of deadlines!

CHAPTER SEVEN

Longing for peace

I like to watch your face turn into shades of bright golden, as the glimmering rays of the morning sun peep in through the bedroom curtains. Your jet black, silky hair eventually appears a tinge of shining brown, and I cannot help but admire how adorable you look as you continue to sleep like a teenage boy, tired after school and play.

I like how your rough but warm hands make their grip on mine, as we walk mindlessly through the half-empty streets in the evening, as little children play soccer at a distance, and aged folk form opinions on our college love.

I like how you carefully scan through all the flavors as we stand in front of that ice-cream truck, and scratch your head asking me about my choice, even though my conventional reply would always be chocolate. I like how in the past few months I've happily settled for butterscotch, and you've made me reconsider my obsession for bonbon.

I like how you stare at me lovingly, as you slowly smoke your cigarette, and the rain keeps pouring cats and dogs outside. As the chilly gusts of wind cause my lips to tremble in cold, and hands almost feel frozen, your warm breath and that sudden bear hug, feels oh so comforting, as I thank my stars for this kind of intimacy.

Each time we sit together gulping down glasses of whiskey or vodka, I eagerly wait to get submerged in intoxication, only so I can blurt out every little way in which your love makes me feel butterflies in my belly. I know that alcohol never dominates you, and even though at times it can surely annoy, there is a certain kind of fun however in spitting out the stupidest of feelings and baby love as your man simply stares at you sober, absorbing all of the ways in which you express your affection for him.

I like how you occasionally rebuke me whenever needed, as I make a face, embarrassed to be admonished in public. But then you'd slowly whisper to me, and tell me it's just so I learn what's right, and for a moment I spot a confidant in you.

I like how you'd pull me close in public, to ensure I'm safe and protected, and somehow my face would blush red as I'd watch my dream boy do it all for me. In the nights when we'd talk about friends, family, and life, and I'd be the only one to keep blabbering like a parrot, since I talk way too much, I'd let out a coy smile as I'd watch you close your eyes every now and then, struggling hard to fight away the inevitable rush of sleep.

I like how you unnecessarily burden yourself with the silliest thought of what I should have for breakfast, even when you would battle with your hunger as your stomach would wrench in pain, and you'd keep quiet about it so gracefully. I like how your little eyes flood with tears of love, whenever I joke about leaving you. Even though I hate to see you in pain, those tears remind me of how deep our connection has grown up to be.

I'd record you when you eat, I'd record you when you laugh, but I'd rather keep my phone aside and watch you like a crazy romantic when you stand facing the mirror, and fix up your oh so gorgeous hair, and I grin from ear to ear like an idiot mad in love.

As this night marks the third day of us not talking to each other, I do open up the recordings to hear your voice, and watch your face, but nothing can really make up for this empty void that has been existing inside of me. A voice inside me says it craves for your presence.

Even though I fight, and scream obscenities, I'm sure you would know the weakest of men hide behind their anger. Anger acts like a shield that camouflages all insecurities, but alas it doesn't realize the extent to which it can cause damage. I know I've caused brutal damage, but I know it's only me who can clear up the mess that I have created.

All I'm in need of is a 'yes' that is wrapped in reassurance, and a smile that is willing to welcome me back into your world, and make me your centre.
I'll rather wait than let go.

• 15 •

CHAPTER EIGHT

A note

Sixteen years is undeniably a very long time to speak of, but regardless I fortunately concluded that I could withstand the most tumultuous times, with a smile that was unbelievable, and a demeanor that was flawless. It was as if I was teaching myself to somehow thrive inside a conflicted and brutally damaged soul, while eventually transforming it into a resistant and indestructible self, which at some point I knew I would refuse to believe in. The irony of it all was the interesting fact that I was capable of stopping the monster without turning myself into one. Although I had fallen victim to hatred and cold-hearted sentences expressing themselves through violent actions, I still take pride in saying that empathy and benevolence yet keep me company. I guess those sixteen years weren't just never-ending months of sorrow and unwanted despair, but a genuinely long enough time to mould me into a tougher self that could stay put through everything, even though slowly withering away.

Sixteen years later, I stumble upon a kind of love that makes me believe in the possibility of permanence, and the achievability of absolute happiness. Sixteen years later I'm told by a stranger that I am worthy of a love that consumes me, and I am capable of being loved generously. Even though the shadows of danger were dancing somewhere in the backdrop of it all, a sliver of hope somehow shown in me, and I held his hand firmly, as if allowing myself to accept the idea that I too was deserving of another chance at living. Walking down the memory lane, I did recall the innumerable days when my hope stemmed up from nothing but lighted candles and habitual prayers, all directed to someone who had never paid me a visit when I looked up to the stars and sobbed silently. Even though I knew none but He had heard me, I had never heard him speak a word that would console me. But exactly sixteen years later I reckon, it was only He who watched it all, and waited for my time to come. Maybe all that emotional outpour was necessary for me to embrace supreme bliss when it came to me.

But then again, my insides were still raw. The wounds are still fresh, and the heart still aces at nights when the stars refuse to show. Every truth somehow hints at a lie, even when there couldn't be the slightest possibility. Every act of acceptance feels like a façade that would soon fade away. Every word of assurance sounds like fabricated half-truths. Even when I know this love is the poetic kind that they write in books, how do I refill the empty void that now screams of insecurities and distrust because of what happened over a period of sixteen long years? Even though I had picked myself up and walked through it all to stand here today, how do I confidently claim that I'm yet again ready to fight a new battle, without knowing what awaits me? Someone told me it takes time to gather yourself. What I fear however is what if it takes me longer than how long the other person is willing to wait for?

I have moved past the falsified version of love that tormented me for sixteen long years, and that I am certain of. But how do I lay faith in the sudden version of unconditional love, knowing all I've ever gotten in return is abandonment? The never-ending fear still holds me back each night, but this time I know I'll conquer it. My only reinforcement is time, and I hope this man offers it to me in abundance, for what I fear the most is to be left stranded with a broken heart, only for not being able to gather myself within the said amount of time. no wonder now I know why the world complains of deadlines!

Reflections

To fall in love is a universal experience. If your stomach twists and turns unusually when you see them, if your heart beat fastens its pace when they look you in the eye, and if you feel your blood rushing furiously as they let out a smile, then you must know it's love that has consumed your senses, as you reckon you're no longer able to push it back. Falling in love is that easy.

What's nightmarish however is whether that someone loves you back; whether they spot the shine in your eyes as your cheeks flush red, whether they catch sight of the momentary crease in your skin extending from both sides of your nose to the corners of the mouth as you struggle to hide the smile, and whether they sense the heightened rush of emotions in you as you get all jittery and begin feeling butterflies inside. And if they do discover it all, and sense a similar desire, then it's nothing but two lovers destined to unite. And love happens just like that- a kind of love that is driven by unfathomable passion, the consistent and overwhelming urge to see each other every day of the week, and the irresistible impulses that drive you bonkers. A love that offers you adventure and makes you step out of the ordinary, is what pushes you to crave for it every passing day. Love intoxicates your soul to the extent that it becomes an arduous challenge to live a day without them.

I had become the fortunate victim of such a love almost three months back, and ever since not a day has passed when I didn't succumb to the cruelties of distance. Surely a favored generation, we need not wait for handwritten letters to arrive, neither do we have to strive for phone calls. However when the ever-increasing farness and the overwhelming burden of assignments keep you within bounds and confines me to limits, then how do I tame that furiously beating heart inside of me that shrieks in agony as it grieves for your absence? How do I teach it to not get nostalgic each time a day of togetherness comes to a close? How do I reason with the foolishly anxious mind of mine that just can't think of anything else but you? How do I convince my longing soul that it must not give up on hope? How do I summon all my strength to force it all into submission, when the soaring emotions in me are just not willing to listen? The day you come up with an answer to it all, I shall finally teach my heart to love in limits.

CHAPTER TEN

"Our" love

Many of us are hopeless romantics, always looking for the 'fairytale love' that we see in movies, and read in conventional and idealistic poetry. Even though barely a possibility, we still like to believe in the idea that someday such a love would be achievable. People like us just can't think of a life that is deprived of romantic love, and the thrill of commitment, even when we are ourselves on the edge of life, so much so that we are certain one wrong step would cause us to fall off the cliff, and it all would come falling apart. Herein lays the baffling irony, because even after knowing it all full well, we are more than willing to risk it all because somehow we wish to make believe in the idea of chances. It's a 'hit or miss' situation, and yet we embrace the daunting challenge whole heartedly. I wonder how many of us would be willing to take on such uncertain challenges when it came to equally important matters, for instance career opportunities, and establishing a stable future. Maybe this is exactly why the world says that love blinds you. So much so, that you fail to ascertain the pros and cons, and all the missed signals simply look like ongoing chances for betterment. Maybe that is what lets people like us to continue to be overwhelmed and swooning over a kind of love, which we have certainly attempted to equate with the perfected and enhanced version depicted in books, and films. Some among us are waiting to start afresh. We have never been told that we were the reason for someone's lost sleep, weirdly interesting dreams, heightened rush of adrenaline, jitter and overwhelming excitement, or even why someone never missed a class, or skipped the morning assembly. We were so oblivious of what it meant to be spending time with the special someone, that we would bury our heads in shame if they came specifically to see us. We would be drowning in the sea of awkwardness when a friend would catch someone staring at us, and smiling. People like us would grow up to be so conscious of ourselves in terms of appearance and confidence, that at times we would look into the mirror and pause for a moment to point out the visible flaws that might've kept them away. And just then, a friend would come to hold your hand, and look you in the eye, with an assuring smile and a firm grip, to tell you that you're perfect just the way you are, only so you continue to hold on to the sliver of hope within, that someday someone would be eager to see you right after the morning sun disturbs their peaceful slumber. We do wait for that 'romantic love' but at the same time watch it co-exist with the other aspects of life, as the saying of 'go with the flow' floods our conscience, and we know we're out of choices.

There is this other group of people who are now used to falling in love, watching it eventually escalate and surpass all boundaries, and then suddenly find them doomed by the very idea of it. These people have taken care of all possible and necessary requirements to somehow try to stay afloat, as the surges of love continue to grow wild. They started out as insecure lovers, beginning to acknowledge the fact that love was a two-way process, and trust comes with a boost in confidence. They begin as half-hearted individuals who are yet to love themselves, and therefore tend to constantly rely on their partner for support. They do not realize that the only true source of their mental peace is they themselves, and their quality and ability of manifesting the same, through self-care. Yet some others find love when they are already struggling to move past their existing trauma. Then there are those who watch the spark gradually fizzle out, as the beginning had been way too intense. So much so, that now all there's left is consequent obsession, which ultimately tarnishes the essence of the bond. These people have survived through so much, that the slightest glimmer of hope ends up lightening up their faces, although now they are governed by the constant fear of abandonment, or the worry of the past repeating itself.

While on the one hand, some are naïve lovers waiting to be loved and willing to give in their everything, only so they do not end up losing, and being left alone once again, the others on the other hand are already exhausted beyond possibilities, and fail to whole-heartedly embrace the new kind of love that comes to them. While giving in everything already, turns you into a foolish lover blinded by the idea of unconditional intimacy and fondness, restricting yourself on the other hand makes you yearn for acceptance and acknowledgement, even as you teach yourself to love within boundaries. The only solution to this inevitable conflict therefore, is tremendous amount of patience, and the willingness to help make it work, no matter how longer it takes.

But one shall also not forget that we are part of a fast moving world, where people barely have the time to take a pause and breathe. We certainly are a group of heightened individuals who lack the ability to have unwavering patience in them, and the willingness to wait for change. If love demands patience and readiness, then perhaps the contemporary world is yet not ready for "our" kind of love.

CHAPTER ELEVEN

Behind the scenes

You were that uninvited guest in my once hollow heart that was bereft of promising lines, and any ray of a new sunshine. Gradually however, I watched you become a permanent resident of it, and eventually making it your abode. Unknowingly, I did give a nod to that unheard agreement, and just like that, you turned from a tenant to the impressive but capable owner of my then fragile but healing heart. Some four months back, when you were just a name to me, I never envisioned a bond with you, that would be strong enough to let our vulnerable selves collide yet survive so gracefully. Slowly but steadily, I began to live my life the way I was meant to. All of the sudden, the unfolding of an ordinary love felt like an exceptional show of affection, perhaps because I was never exposed to the true essence of intimacy, and fondness.

I don't think you would ever realize the weight of the ascendancy of good that you continue to have, over the evil in me. You've not just settled in the deepest reaches of my heart, but also taken up residence in the empty spaces that were left inside of me, and my relationships. You didn't just become a potential lover, and a crazy romantic, but the only bosom buddy, my confidant, and the safe place I'd return to whenever I'd be tormented by the ravages of time. As and when I grew up into this scarred young woman, deeply disturbed by the downsides of friendships, family, and line of work, I correspondingly also envied happy relationships, growing friendships, and exciting family reunions, wishing someday I'd see the same in mine. Somehow in the span of these few months, you showed me that was still a possibility.

In the smallest of moments that I got to spend with you, I very proudly express that I have had the chance to rebuild better and matchless memories that can never be compared. It has been a journey of both growth and lessons. I learnt to find happiness in speaking to father on call without sensing any discomfort in myself. I learnt to appreciate every slightest act of kindness by a stranger. I learnt to save up, so I could afford my needs and not spoil myself with irrelevant materialistic possessions. I learnt to look forward to meeting my family. I learnt to take a step back and work to build a life that would serve both of us in the best of ways. I learnt to differentiate between faces that once looked so familiar to me. I learnt to speak for myself, and speak on the face of those who constantly bogged me down with their sharp, prickly sentences that pierced my soul frequently. You taught me so much that over these few months; I could feel my inner self transform- into someone who now wished for growth.

I knew there was an unmatched comfort in the sound of heavily pouring rain, as I would sit alone and watch the sky turn soft grey. But I never knew the beauty of silence when I sat at the same spot holding your hand, as the chilly wind caused my insides to shiver just a little, and the rain grew heavier. The gargantuan trees would swing from left to right, as though signaling the advent of a thunderstorm. Yet everything would feel so tranquil, and I'd develop a love for monsoon. I knew English music was one of my greatest choices, but never imagined I'd someday build myself a playlist of Punjabi beats, and catch myself grooving to its rhythm. I knew I was heartbroken and brutally shattered into a zillion pieces, but I never realized the most powerful humans were those who had been broken a thousand times over.

My experiences in this lifetime have made me acknowledge one true thing about the present. And that is, no matter how old you grow up to be, your number of ordeals and extent of suffering shapes you into a level-headed human, who is now much considerate and evolved. And the day I came to know of you, and your encounters with life's most cruelest and deadly battles, I reckoned that you finally declared peace for yourself, as the fresh wounds reminded you of the constant agony. It wasn't that your bruises were healing, but you eventually began to look for effective remedies, rather than addressing the same pain all over again. You still hurt, you still sobbed each night, you still visited the past whenever you could, you still camouflaged your existing trauma with the color of boiling anger, but nevertheless you put on that lively smile, and walked through life with a puffed up chest, knowing full well that someday you'd be completely free. All you had to do was keep looking for the cure, and one fine morning, you'd not have to look anymore. Peace would consume you entirely. That was when I cognized that even though I was in love with a man a year younger than me, he lived a life that had been much older than mine, and his heart was like the ripened mango that grew even sweeter, after months of being left alone to mature, as the glimmering sun and the heavy winds watched it grow nice and firm. The pit at the center is not tough anymore, but soft and tender. That was when I knew, that whatever comes next in life, I want you to run your fingers through my hair, hold my face in your somewhat rough but warm hands and look me in the eyes, plant a kiss on my forehead as you read my mind with devotion, and pull me close to your chest, as if reassuring me that this is going to last forever.

The common perils of every bond of love translate into distance, lack of time, and gradually diminishing communication. But with you in my life, I have begun to realize why some of it is inevitably a part of our communion. To speak in your words, this is our time to build ourselves the incredibly amazing future that would see us as partners bonded by the promise of eternal love. You and I have a few years at hand, no matter the inevitable distance, zeroing down of communication, or the paucity of quality time. And in this few months, we could make a promise of a lifetime of togetherness, since we're onboard, building ourselves the happy live that we want to live, hand in hand, travelling the world in the brightest colors, and creating newer memories to be added to another album! Life seems so beautiful with you.

They say love is about attachments, a deeper sense of intimacy, and an unparalleled connection between two souls. Love to me however, is all about the readiness and eagerness to work for a shared fate, in which the blues never get a chance to knock on our door again. Love is about giving in everything, so it all lasts forever.

So after it all, it is to you that I say, don't ever talk of leaving your home, that others would call my heart. You've built your space and taken up all rooms, and now you'll have to stay. I'm sure you know the pain of leaving, when the place is drowning with your memories. I'm sure you know how abandoned it feels, when a house is stripped off its family. It would no longer remain a home, but merely an empty place that would reminisce the good times, and hope for you to come back. Just like a family holds on together, even when the world conspires against them, I want you to hold onto me just the same, for now my love for you no longer knows any bounds. It keeps soaring each day, and it would cause me death if someday I'm asked to bottle it all up. I'd look for you in heaven even then, for I know that overwhelming love would still be alive in me. Now tell me, would you still stay?

CHAPTER TWELVE

Existential conflicts

In my twenty-two years of existing as a somewhat traumatized, socially anxious, reticent, and timid adult woman, who has had her fair share of highs and lows in life, I have considered myself fortunate enough to have lived through an incredible amount of significant experiences that have had a crucial role to play in my understanding of relationships. Over the years I have grown up to become a person who acknowledges and fully accepts the idea that the 'maturity' of an individual is what can be gauged through his/her experiences and struggles that they had to endure, throughout their lives. A teenage boy, who has grown up as an abandoned kid in the nearby orphanage, would know about the grief of desertion better than an adolescent who has grown up under the care of overwhelmingly preoccupied guardians. Similarly, an adolescent who has seen dozens of relationships build and break would know about the trauma of heartbreak in a better way, than a naïve young girl in her twenties who is reeling from the culmination of a month-old bond.

One recurring thought that has kept my conscience preoccupied for months now, has been the persistent question of why has pain become an inalienable part of every relationship, so much so that it never subsides but only grows in intensity. I have heard women complain of how they have continued to pour in all their love, by planning out sudden surprises, designing special cakes, doodling cute gift cards, and even taking care of every little activity, and yet get no such gesture as a means of reciprocation. They comprehend it as a 'lack of effort'. On the other hand, I also hear men talking about how they are never understood in ways that they ought to be, which ultimately builds the foundation for an inevitable split as a consequence of eminent conflict. Gradually the process of healing that follows is accompanied by isolation to a point where you begin feeling no one is compatible enough for you. All of it makes me wonder if ending an age-old bond of love has become that easy of a task. Whom do we blame for this unfortunate end, is it the overly loving women who are way too emotionally vulnerable and weak at heart, or is it the emotionally restricted, toughened, and aggressive men who feel forced to strictly adhere to the supposed idea of masculinity?

This is exactly where there develops an urgent need to take into account the societal differences between the two genders. Books have contributed significantly to our understanding of women and how they perform their roles in society, as also how their entire orientation appears to be. Ironically, however, there is little or no discussion around the psychology of men, who are generally and simplistically described as those who need to work to feed a family. We do not know how a man's brain works when he falls in love, or what his brain does when he feels pain and agony. I assume a better understanding of the 'male psychology' would help us look into how their 'lack of effort' unknowingly leads to the end of year-long chapters of love and romance. Since women feel too much, it wouldn't be wrong to suggest that things don't end up on the same page since men feel so little. What one might view as a lack of maturity might in reality be his lack of emotional availability since he is already too cluttered in his head. Therefore it might be wrong to label him as a faulty lover when in actuality he is just a naïve boy who is yet to grow up into a man, who finally has all means to devote equal time to his partner and his goals. Growing up is a steady process, and we simply cannot expect someone to step into the shoes of a man in his late thirties one morning, who has all his priorities sorted and settled.

As surprising as it may sound, studies suggest that men desire more or less the same things that a woman desires from a relationship. Some of these desires stem from the need to feel a deeper sense of connection, effective means of communication, and wanting to be felt and heard, to be listened to. If we go by the general idea that suggests 'women are the most complicated beings to be comprehended fully', the scientific data clears up some air and puts forth the conclusion that men and women are more alike than significantly different when it comes down to their needs and mental orientation. However, one interesting point of difference could be indicative of the fact that men feel the strict need to adhere to the norms of masculinity, which in a way leads them to suppress the emotions necessary for any intimate relationship. The general way in which men are dismissed as 'genetically deficient' beings when it comes to their inability to express themselves entirely, or talk about their innermost troubles openly, makes them avoid communication that is way too intimate and deep. To comprehend this situation, it may be necessary for us to look into how boys are conditioned in their societies since their childhood, and how such conditioning shapes their minds in a way that they grow up to be unable to handle conflict in a relationship. No wonder, this is why we say women tend to be ahead of the curve when it comes to maturity as compared to that of men. This is probably because as women, we are taught to be accountable and responsible for our actions, be emotionally available, excel in child care, and be the submissive self who is always soft-hearted and benevolent. Unlike these women, men are simply made familiar with the idea that someday they would have to hold a job well enough to sustain their families and become the protective guard that can never break even in times of adversity. The emphasis on building them as such rigid personalities becomes so high that they are seldom told to share their fears or emotions, express hurt, or vent it out. Rather, anger develops as a defense mechanism through which they display their weakest versions through violent actions, deluded by the idea that it makes them appear strong. The constant need to not express any pain, even when they feel it in extremes, builds up their ego which becomes way too adamant to ever accept defeat.

Beginning in boyhood, men are expected to try and conform to the societal norms of masculinity. Consequentially therefore, men grow up to control their innermost emotions and make sure to not appear 'vulnerable' at any cost. Failure is sinister to them, as society enforces upon them the need to build and feed a family, so much so that a man staying at home and looking after the kids appears to be an idealistic situation. To them, earning enough is not just a testimony to their ability to feed a family but also the point of validation that they can now be viewed as a potential life partner. Therefore the pressure to build a stable future is such that the constant frightening concern alienates them from the reality. The perturbing thought of coming at par with his social circle who already have the biggest positions in reputed companies, the upcoming shame from the society, family, and partner in case of failure at work, the inevitable frustration due to not being able to open up about the deepest emotions, and the overpowering burden of looking after his family and taking control of all responsibilities, can break a man so much so that he barely finds any time to reflect at himself, rather than focusing on how he could contribute to a healthy love life. Different men have different ways and strategies to cope up with such a depressing and demanding phase. Some move out of their shells and decide to communicate, irrespective of the outcomes. Some find solace in distancing themselves from the world, and hustling in silence. Some turn to alcohol, misinterpreting it as an effective solution to all their misery.

This is however not to suggest that 'benevolent sexism' or attributing maturity to a specific gender is the best thing to do. Describing boys as immature and girls as mature may lead women to accept the indecent and inappropriate behaviors of men, with the perception that 'men will be men'. Likewise, men would never learn to take responsibility for their actions, and rather would justify themselves as "this is how I am".

Therefore in every romantic relationship, the conflicted psyche of men and the aspect of benevolent sexism, that works in continuing the inevitable conflict eventually drains the bond of love and mutual understanding. While women do every possible thing to keep the spark going and alive, men's inability to stay consistent eventually washes away all efforts. In this evident conundrum, none is to be blamed for their individual troubles, but the solution lies in mutual cooperation. If the love for the significant other has made you fall to your knees, move beyond your boundaries, embrace change, experience intimacy, visualize a happy future infused with success and excitement, and has made you dance with joy, then that same love is worth saving.

Underneath the differential conditioning of the two genders, there is a child who desires love, and wishes someone to be okay with them when they aren't winning. Men want women to talk to them about their day (just like women want the same for themselves). Men utterly despise the idea of dependency when it comes to emotional support. This is because such a form of dependency would make him feel the burden of constantly presenting himself as your next 'boost' rather than his authentic self. In such a situation, women would be more susceptible to criticizing their partners. The solution therefore lies in accepting yourself and embracing self-love.

In fear of stigmatization, most men tend to avoid communicating their vulnerable thoughts. Hence, if a man speaks about his insecurities, he needs to be taken seriously and questioned for his concerns, so much so that he feels the joy of effective communication, and the level of intimacy further enhances. A man would love to be viewed as a real person who is (for a moment) free of control and agendas for the day. Deep down therefore, the wants and desires of both the partners in every relationship are way too similar. The problem lies in believing that support is demanded by only either of them. The social requirement of men to work as emotionally reliant beings often makes them unable to speak about their needs from a relationship. They constantly 'supervise' the signs of potential conflict in their partners, the result of which leads them to blame themselves for their failure. Over time, the extent of them avoiding conflict becomes so much that eventually they cede from trying. It is necessary for us women to realize that men value independence more than intimacy. And therefore the constant need for time and space is necessary to let them breathe and not feel suffocated by any bond. Men demand security and certainty just as we do, and that comes from approval of him and his goals. Trust builds up security, and that alone is enough to overcome the worst of hurdles.

To put it simply, for a relationship to work, we want the boys to become better men for us. And that can only be done if we consider them similar to us, and in need of the same reassurances that we yearn for. If love is to stay, the two individuals have to know that it's only supposed to get better. The 'efforts' start from trying to gauge what's going on inside, rather than imposing labels that categorize them as 'immature', 'toxic', or 'cheats'.

Loving you has been dicey!

Walking down the same old deserted street, I realize I am no longer the same old me. Although the neighborhood looked familiar, and a strong gust of wind brought back month old memories that I had been saving myself from, I could sense a part of me no longer existed like it used to once. I look ahead and continue walking, foolishly wondering if I'd spot you at a distance, waiting for me to come hold your hand. I can feel a teardrop escape my already moist eyes, but this time I don't sense any need to wipe it off. I'm too fragile to withstand the overwhelming outpour of intense emotions. I can smell meat being cooked somewhere, but nothing delights me anymore. Perhaps it is the sour realization that this time I'd have to finish it all alone. Young lovers in and around the corners makes my heart palpitate, as if I had summoned anxiety to settle in. I look at them smile at each other, as they rest their heads upon their lover's chest, and an empty void within me yearns for attention. I just cannot fathom if it is the affection that I crave, or is it the simple assurance of having you right beside me whenever I was close to crumbling. Isn't it utterly unfair that you spent the longest of days and nights with me, fulfilling every fantasy that I ever dreamt of, only to turn them into memories that haunt me as nightmares each time I force my eyes shut? Isn't it insanely cruel of you to touch me in the ways that no one ever could; only so one morning I'd plead my stars to let me feel your warmth for one last time? Isn't it brutal of you to talk of a shared future in which I'd be the hot-tempered mother of your kids, only to leave me midway wondering if our love had been so delicate? Let me tell you just so you know, falling in love hasn't been easy. I knew it would be one rollercoaster ride, but I was prepared to embrace the thrills. Waking up next to you each morning soothed my senses beyond your imagination. I'd only care about keeping happy, because everything else magically fell into place. All the random cups of tea by the roadside stalls, silly comments hurled at strangers, slurping spicy noodles at the same old shop (because you knew I'd never opt for anything else), smoking cigarettes in the breezy evenings, exchanging playlists while you'd mock my tastes, teasing me with your friends while I would blush and hide my face, giving me life lessons that shaped me into a woman of power, all those late night rides while the rain poured down on us, kissing underneath the stars while your creepy neighbor watched us silently- I never wished for these to turn into faint memories that I'd narrate to a friend at three in the morning, with bright red eyes devoid of sleep, as I'd rub them time and again, and speak through my tears. Isn't it heartless of you to lift me up like a princess and give me a glimpse of the world we both could inhabit, only to suddenly decide to drop me from such a height so I fall into rock bottom, and never see you again? Is that what love is all about- quitting when there's no meeting point? I still wonder.

Just a week back, I found myself around some great company- young men who were equally broken into shreds and pieces, yet stood through to carry on with the life they've envisioned to live for. They watched me fall but stood right there to pick me up. They then pushed me harder so I'd fall even worse, but then asked me to pick myself up. They showed me what love felt like, but they also told me about the powers it came with. They warned me that love could build you, but break you too. They shared with me their biggest secret- that no matter how happy you saw a man to be, every man carries a lonely heart that longs for acceptance- the acceptance of a man who could crumble at times, who could collapse anytime whenever the load of responsibilities would weigh heavy on him. They taught me that life helps us grow, life helps us understand. It is the toil and struggle of life that gives us the perfect shape. They taught me that heartbreak is universal.

But even then there are nights when I jump back into the thoughts of us, letting myself weep profusely as my heart slowly accepts the absence that you've left behind. I still feel empty and wasted, I still feel devoid of emotions. I still look for love in every boy that smiles back at me, I still look for assurance in every man that embraces me. I still think of heartbreak when someone confesses his liking for me. I still search for you when someone mentions love to me. If not as my Prince Charming who'd ride his white horse to carry me to his castle, won't you ever meet me at the other end of the river, as a friend I'd never want to part ways with? If not love and the apocalyptic romance, can we not sit on the moist grass and simply talk about how once we blissfully enjoyed existing together? Can we not cry in each other's arms, as we'd barely be able to breathe, until one of us cracks a joke and both of us break into laughter, only to realize we still love each other like we used to?

CHAPTER FOURTEEN

Grief and acceptance

For the first time ever, in all these years, I have carefully watched every day pass by, from the rise of the morning sun to the settling in of the night sky. I've faithfully kept a count of the number of days in this month, and for once in life I've reckoned that a month long time can feel like a decade long story. I consciously observed the diverse set of diversions that exist, to let you temporarily dissociate from the turmoil of the real world. I've spoken to people- both known and unknowns, only to feel what it felt to have someone's presence around. For once in all this time, I'm watching pain settle in with me. I can see how adamant it is to not leave me on my own terms; it is a lot more stubborn this time as it remains constant. It visits me in my sleep, greets me every morning, watches me forcefully chomp down tasteless meals, consumes me entirely as and when I try to look elsewhere as it clouds my vision, it clogs my heart with all sorts of impatience, yearning, and dread. Last night I took a seat under the starlit sky, as I breathed heavily, and the freezing wind punished me. I took my time to settle in, and let my conscience discern that I was slowly disintegrating, piece by piece. That was when my mind traced back the root of all the pain to you. Just like I said, pain was everywhere. My music reminded me of the existing pain, the places I loved to visit, inflicted brutal pain upon me, the people I once laughed with, jogged my memory with pain. Well wishers told me to wake up with hope, have timely meals, brush and take showers, go for walks, and shake hands with strangers. Probably that was their preferred idea of helping me walk past it all. Having born as an ultimate 'people pleaser', I felt obligated to abide by it all. But I shall tell you the truth now. It isn't much difficult to do the usual, as you've been doing it ever since you were brought to this world. What's difficult however, is to watch the pain co-exist with you, to let it remind you of how everything pulled you down to your knees as you sobbed and whimpered when no one noticed, constantly questioning yourself how you couldn't do enough even after spending nearly all the twenty-four hours in thinking of all the possible ways in which you could show them how down you were for them. What's difficult however is to be absolutely unable to stop yourself from returning to the slowest hits, and not crumbling apart, as every word hits home. What is difficult is to coerce yourself to continue breathing, even when survival seems the toughest challenge ever since your inception. No one talks of how you are supposed to erase all the blissful memories from the mind and soul, in just a span of months or even years. When love is true and real, nothing really vanishes ever. It stays, but eventually makes you realize that you can't really help yourself. But what if I really want to help myself? What if I'm still desperate for a reason to run back? What if I'm still knee deep for the connection that we shared with each other? If love can turn to pain in four months, why can't that same pain melt away into love after years?

Ever since you decided to remove me from even the sidelines, you have no idea how excruciatingly painful it has been for me to continue surviving with forceful breathing. You don't have the slightest clue in the world about how insanely tormenting it has been for me to look for the most foolish reasons only to be able to wake up alive each morning. You don't realize how helpless it feels to mourn and whimper, crouched up in the corner of the room until I start to choke, and struggle for air. You don't understand how every random street, every delicacy, every picture; every travel has now become an enemy that enjoys watching me collapse every now and then. When did I give you so much power to tear me up mercilessly? Why did I fall so truly, madly, and deeply for your ways? Perhaps because I wasn't used to seeing the best in life?

For the first time in my life, I wish I never had the ability to retain memories. One small accident in love and an inevitable unconsciousness for life perhaps would've been my cure.

CHAPTER FIFTEEN

How are you doing?

These days I get to be enlightened by innumerable individuals-surprisingly the ones who have never had the slightest chance of peeking into the deepest reaches of my soul, that clearly screams of a deep-rooted and intense past. It appears funny to me, but I nod to their words regardless. People watch you disintegrate with time, and instantly assume you've seldom made an effort to gather yourself as a whole. What is even funnier is how they don't realize that even the bravest of soldiers lose in constant wars. Nevertheless each new day, I watch people come to me with newer theories and philosophies about life and love, and I say nothing but smile.

Currently, I've been listening to this playlist titled "Acoustic Melodies", while I'm writing yet another letter to you, absolutely unsure if it will ever reach you, and if you'd turn the pages to read through. The song that is playing on my phone right now is called "Poison and Wine by The Civil Wars". Do you remember when I played it for you on the speakers, the day we completed just a month of togetherness but it seemed like a major milestone we both had achieved? Do you remember how I had decorated that entire room of yours with golden lights, and made you a tiny space encircled with heart-shaped candle lights? Do you remember how the previous night you brought me an entire tub of your favorite ice-cream and a big chocolate bar because you said you weren't creative enough to think of any other gift? Do you remember how I had completed the entire set up, and just as I was about to turn on my golden lights, a power outage took over, but you took me in your arms, kissed my forehead, and simply thanked me for all the endeavor?

I wish you could see how I'm smiling like a teenage girl who obsesses over her school time crush, and hopes someday she'd tell him how she wishes for him to hold her hand and look her in the eye, and whisper in her ear that he loves her back.

Well, I was just overwhelmed with curiosity. Do you also remember the evenings when we would sit facing the balcony, with the lights turned off, as you'd hold my hand and stare at me while I would blush and blabber about life? Do you remember the showers we took, and how you'd bathe me with your favorite choice of gel? Do you remember how you'd often take me to that busy market street, where we'd just stroll clueless, only to return home with an ice-cream for me? Do you still remember how you'd cuddle with me every night, after we finished watching the funniest movies on Netflix? D you often get nostalgic about how I'd sit on your lap, and laugh like a silly child, as you'd hold me from behind and suddenly turn me to face you, and kiss me? No, I don't cry anymore when I recall those moments we'd spent together. I reckon you don't appreciate when I cry. You don't like it when you see me fall weak. And hence these days, I don't cry. My heart surely does, but my eyes don't get moist anymore. They're hopeful, and expecting. Even though I know it's tremendously wrong to do, but that small voice inside of me still tells me you'd come someday. I'm certain you will, if not in this life, then surely in the rest that follow. I am certain, I am convinced. Even if you do give a piece of your heart to another woman you stumble upon in the next few years, I know your soul is still reminiscing my memories. You just got the best of me, young man.

How are you doing baby? Do you still wake up past 10 AM? Do you still struggle with your papers, or have you managed to make time? Do you take all your meals, or have you been skipping some? Are you now regularly hitting the gym? I wonder how many women hit on you. Do you stay up in the nights, or have you been getting sound sleep? Do your friends ask you about your health? Do they take you out for a much needed break? Have you erased all our memories that I still cling on to, or does your gallery still have my ugliest pictures? Do you still visit nightclubs, or do they remind you of me? Do you wish I was there to hold you tight when the cold grew intense, or do the fleecy jackets help?

Do you still remind someone to drink water throughout the day, like you used to do to me? Do you get gift cards and little sketches? Have you discarded my gifts that I gave you every month, or do you still keep them somewhere safe? Is my book still with you, or did you pass it on to someone else? Oh dear, I have so many things to ask you, and so much to know of you, if only I would hear from you once.

I hope to wait for your call till my upcoming birthday on the 2nd of February. No matter if you return or don't, I want you to remain the friend who still holds on to all my secrets, and perhaps the only man who had peeked into the deepest reaches of my soul. I'd wait for you on earth; I shall wait for you in heaven. Come see me, the day you feel the world has gotten too big, and you're in need of a safe haven.

CHAPTER SIXTEEN

I'm sending my smiles to you!

Day 15 of writing a letter to you,

Just some twenty minutes ago, I had posted a picture of me online. If only we were still connected, I'm certain you would've smiled looking at it. I smile in that picture. The agonizing beam of the glowing afternoon sun casts a brownish golden tint in my eyes. My pale yellow skin is glistening in the sunshine, as I smile for the picture. My hair feels smooth and healthy, as it rests calmly on my shoulders, unbothered by the wild breeze. I know you'd have been happy to hear about this day, because I made a new friend. I vividly remember how you said, "good people make good friends. You just need to find them". Well, she had always been a bosom buddy, but this afternoon she had been my custodian. She had been a keeper of my little secrets, and the sole witness to my bruised existence. If only a friend of yours would share this picture with you, you'd get to see how lively I look! Yes, I haven't cried. I haven't mourned for your absence. I haven't laid my emotions bare, and I haven't cursed my love for you. On the flipside however, I talked to her about you, and how we'd have been if you had been here with me. The place was infested with lovers of all kinds. For once in all these years, we even spotted a man of around fifty being affectionate with his wife. All of them reminded me of you, and I laughed madly. I laughed recalling how you loathed showing affection in public. I laughed recollecting how you'd ask me to rather 'behave' if I had requested you for a kiss while I lay my head on your thighs. Oh one thing you'd not be much happy about, and that is the choice of music we chose today. We didn't listen to your treasured Punjabi hits, but soft renditions of classic Bollywood. A woman walked up to us, requesting us for a picture with her lover man, to which my friend happily agreed. I shall now tell you how it reminded me of that festive night on the 1st of October, when you walked up to a cold looking, self contained man, with a similar request, and he made us look like some billed platypus having a rough day.

Oh how I missed you today, if only you knew. Your friends no longer talk to me. I thought they had become my friends too, but perhaps four months were not long enough for them to build a bond with me. I never knew friendships were way more vulnerable than thriving hearts. If only they liked me like they used to once, perhaps you could see that I'm doing good. I still smile, and I still pose for pictures. I wore your favorite clothes, and the shoes that you always wanted to get for me. Don't worry, for you won't see me grieve you. I know you wanted me to be a strong woman, and I'm on my way to become one. Perhaps watching me love myself more than I have loved you, would someday bring you back to me. I had a wonderful evening. I hope you did too.

CHAPTER SEVENTEEN

The Night (should've lasted longer!)

It was all very recent, but you would tell me given the seraphic and divine connection that we shared, it just couldn't have been the case. Trust every word that escapes my mouth, for I'm about to serve you blatant honesty. Like any other, you too could call it a 'date' in the conventional sense of the term, but for me however, it had been one of the most blissfully gratifying days that flooded my senses with abundant and irrepressible happiness, and limitless gratitude. It was sometime in mid November when I saw him enter the room with so much confidence and charm. Back in the time, I used to breathe with a heavy heart, and a forceful slumber was my only escape to a miserable existence, and needless to say, I was lying flat on the bed, wearing borrowed clothes that barely fit my size, and somewhat scanned him through my drowsy eyes, as my hair looked a terrible mess, and my face seemed awfully pale. Believe me when I say I felt the butterflies flutter in my stomach, as he took a seat right in front of me, letting out the most charming smile that I had come across in big time. I hurriedly but excitedly got up, and as if struggling hard to look somewhat tolerable and acceptable, I rubbed my eyes and settled my hair, only so he would just not disgust me and that smile would remain. You could call it my social consciousness, but I hadn't reckoned why it happened. I found myself tremendously attracted to his way of being; there was just something about the way he existed. He looked calm and serene, his cheeks were round and fluffy, and his eyes had a different kind of shine, perhaps the sparkle of curiosity, and his tiny lips made me want to run my fingers through them. Yes, I had managed to take a mental note of every single characteristic that described his charm, so much so that I had to remind myself time and again that love doesn't happen in seconds. It takes time to blossom and mature. However, given that I read abundant poetry and old-school romance novels, something in me also hinted at 'love at first sight' being a closer possibility. All thanks to my then bosom buddy, who seldom failed to include me in conversation, and I found myself blushing every now and then, while I just stared at him in awe as he continued to speak about his past lovers and personal interests. I'm certain and convinced that he had noticed all of it, and as I type this, I can feel a soaring embarrassment in me. Yet I wouldn't call myself guilty, because had he not sensed how he was driving me bonkers, we wouldn't have ever had a second chance to build memories on the 14th of December, 2022.

We spoke for as long as we could, until his best friend from school decided to intrude our happy little bonding session with his not so nice but deceivingly good looking lover. I saw a sudden shift in communication, and unknowingly it did make me envy that woman, because all of the sudden, she had his most attention, and the sound of her laughter made me want to scream in sheer annoyance. So as you would rightly assume, in just about a few minutes I decided to walk out of the room and ask my heart to calm its beating. What if I was falling for him? He would surely not want a homeless looking kid, who sulked the whole day in the corner of the room, listening to sad songs on a loop, to become his honeysuckle. Just as I was talking to my heart and the inner me to deal with the situation effectively, he popped out of nowhere asking why I was outside. Boom! That empty-headed, gullible heart of mine jumped in joy, thinking something was in the air. That evening, we went out for Belgian Waffles and even though my hopes were down, my stars were merciful towards me. We came back home in his car, and although he didn't hold my hand (while I was desperate like a fish out of water struggling to keep alive), I had been praying all throughout that this company isn't our last.

Nevertheless, I had waited for as long as two weeks for him to ask me out (which he never did until I asked him to come see me, because I now couldn't wait any longer) and that was how the 'date' that you'll might call it, came to materialize on the 14th of December, just a day prior to my not so miserable but clearly heartbreaking present.

Although I knew that he purely admired my physical appearance, a part of me still yearns for him to see me for whom I am, and someday love me like he would just not want to let me go. That evening, you could see me hurriedly dress up and literally sprint in the direction of the subway station. Upon reaching, I saw him wait in his car, looking ever so mesmerizing. He surely hadn't noticed how I looked, but I foolishly scanned him through the corner of my eye. As if in response to that, he leaned forward to embrace me, and as soon as I reciprocated, I knew my heart had left my chest. Something about this man just wanted me to let go of all my curtailed emotions, and let them flow.

After dinner (oh how I pleaded thy Lord that he'd do nothing but sit and stare me down, and eventually feel things, but he just wouldn't, and instead would blabber about aliens, work, science, and love), he took me for a drive to India Gate, and from there, to a place I'm surely not forgetting in years to come. This man (the man I was already so crazy for) had planned the whole evening out, so much so that he had booked us a room at a five-star hotel, post all the lip-smacking food and wholesome drive, as Bryan Adams and Backstreet Boys played on the speakers. The hotel windows lend us a glimpse into the airport, and the huge bed and massive bathtub were just the icing on the cake. That night, his kiss didn't feel like a random peck on the lips by a stranger, but the warmth and affection of an age-old lover. His cuddles helped me calm myself down, as for the first time in a long time; sleep hadn't been 'forceful'. More so, I didn't have to light up a cigarette or gulp down whiskey to laugh and let go of the misery in me. I yet don't know what it meant to him, but when we made love, I felt so complete, so in love. It was after a long time, that my smile came from the heart and not from my curving lips.

I wonder if he would speak to me again. I wonder if he would see me again (the weekend already looks so dull and unhappy). I wonder if the memories that we made (discussing life and love while eating at an aesthetically pleasing café, walking out in the cold at an isolated street under a starlit sky, vibing to Hindi and English playlists and Enrique Iglesias, making love like we desired each other's company, sitting in the bathtub in silence as he held my hair so they won't get wet, talking till five in the morning and confessing that we feel a connection) would just stay as random experiences in his heart, or does he miss me already, like I miss him? I wonder if he too is dying to speak to me, like I am. If there's a thing about life and lemons, I'd like to make myself a lemonade (just like he tells me), as soon as I get my hands on them.

I know what I did was a mistake that isn't easy to be forgiven. But if his mind settles and he realizes that I wasn't myself when it all happened, and he speaks to me again to tell me he'd hold me the same like he did that night, I am certain I'd drift to sleep smiling, because my heart would feel at peace. If only he knows how badly this space yearns for him.

CHAPTER EIGHTEEN

Am I falling in love again?

As a naïve young man who is yet to decipher my inner self, only so he can boldly claim my heart, tonight is your time for I'm about to enlighten you with stories that have written down my existence. If you trust yourself as a careful listener, consider it a test of your potential as one. May I also mention, that although you've repeatedly reminded me of your non-judgmental character, tonight I ask for it? You must listen to all that my heart has held on to, ever since my eyes met yours, and how it has struggled since to carefully note down every detail and feel every emotion, before it is prepared to set out for a new adventure, which someday might also lead us to wake up next to each other, not as plain romantic lovers, but as partners bonded by the ring of love.

You ask me if it is love that I feel for you. Surely, it is a strong emotion, but I choose to ask you, what do you know of love? What do you think it is? Tonight let me tell you how a hopeless romantic and a devoted lover as me think it to be. Love to me is the soothing comfort you feel as you lay your head against his chest, after a rigorous day at work. Love to me is when you look at him smiling, and you know it's a good day. Love to me is when you collapse every minute, but he is willing to pick you up again. Love to me is when it's just the howling winds, and a peaceful lane devoid of people, as the birds circle the clear blue horizon, and suddenly nothing seems colorless but full of life, soulful. Love to me is when there is joy in silence, with him by your side. Love to me is when you cry, and loathe, as you snort and your nose turns red, and your eyes hurt from all the tears, and he still sits in silence watching you, for you're still a child in his eyes. Love to me is when your failures don't scare him, and tells you they are the stepping stones, and that he'd walk alongside you. Love to me is the realization, that this man is my refuge, and the day the world caves in on me, he would be waiting on the other side, with a reassuring smile. Love to me, is the faith that amidst all the worst and dread, he would never abandon me, for we are all we have for each other.

You may wonder what makes me different. You see, these words and paragraphs aren't my way of making you fall for my naïve and teenaged heart, but a conscious attempt of mine to let you see the spent soul in me that still longs for a man like you. Think of me as an unfortunate child who loves like an artist loves his art, or the ether loves the rain, yet was never exposed to the pure form of affection that is unfiltered, selfless, patient, and liberal. Think of me as the mislead lover who thought it was real whenever a random man gave her the least possible. Think of me as an exhausted little one, who still longs for a love that never abandons her when she leaves her heart bare. Think of me as the personification of permanence, and I promise to never deceive you, for I know the pain of betrayal, just like a soldier knows the hurt of wounds in a battle.

You see I wasn't born as a crazy romantic. However I knew love drove you crazy. Although you do feel your heart pounding when his face resembles sheer divinity, what keeps you holding on to them is how you catch yourself smiling whenever they smile. I had a 'first time' when someone said he loved me. But as I grew up, I reckoned not everyone realizes what love really is. Either it happens only once, or it doesn't fade away in a few months. That was the day I discerned that attraction was not love. Real love never ends, it either exists somewhere in the corner of your heart, or consumes you entirely. If today, you don't love the same, it was never love to begin with.

The day you spoke to me, I didn't pay heed to your words, and how they beautifully escaped your soft lips, and sounded like music to my ears. What I rather was attentive towards, is how grown you were as a person with emotions. I would rather confess that I did want to kiss you, but my racy and disobedient heart had other plans. It demanded patience and guided attention. It was immensely curious to test your *endeavors, and it wanted to affirm whether you were the man I had dreamt of as a teenage kid. I can't tell if love had already begun to bloom, but I am certain the foundations were laid. To know of your being, I never needed a zillion hours. You seemed so crystalline to me, I could read you through your eyes, and write you with your words. You surely are a curious man, and I wouldn't shy away from saying that it did pull me towards you, but not entirely. I sensed a similarity in our pain. I sensed a resemblance in our personalities. You were tired, and I was too. Was it time that we needed each other? That dull-witted heart screamed a 'yes!', but I rebuked it in response. "Patience", I reminded myself, and continued to test you in words. And just like that, days would pass by, and you would occasionally write to me, but you never spoke to me. Your fingers typed countless phrases, but your heart kept silent, as if cautious of any colossal damage. And I'd smile, realizing how you resemble me so well. Yet, you see, I am an author. And although not all readers are writers, all writers certainly read. And I read through your utterances. Although in the initial days, it hurt me to see you admire my appearance and not my soul; I questioned myself asking how you could anyway, when it was scarred by the ravages of time. But that was until one blissful evening, you told me you wanted me to stay. I vividly recall myself blushing beyond limits, merely staring at my phone's screen, as you continued to type in intervals. My face would flush red, and my grin wouldn't stop, as I constantly covered my face with my right hand, foolishly imagining you standing in front of me, watching me go crimson for you! And so my love, the scene was set, the script was written, and the final edit was eagerly awaited for. And it all came to materialize on the 14th of December, the night I just didn't want to let go of you.*

That night I was certain my intuitions had not lied. The Universe was giving me another chance to let go of all my miseries, and be blissfully in love with you, truly, madly, deeply. But now is the time I tell you that I come with a disclaimer. Tell me dear love, how do you heal a bruise that has become black with time? Do you think the bare minimum would suffice, or extra care is demanded when situations grow worse? I don't ask you to be my physician and write me prescriptions for the rest of my life to follow, but if I may, cant I ask you to be that aid that would be there for me, whenever the pain grew severe? If you fall a hundred times, I'd pick you a thousand times. If love is a poem, I am the poet. If love is a song, I am the singer. If love is an illness, I am the patient. If love is an accident, I am the victim. If love is a muse, I am the dreamer. If love is an art, I am the painter. So if to me, love is you, I am your beloved. I have never fancied abandonment, and of that I'm certain. But if tonight I decide to make you my home, would you choose to reside in it? I'm in two minds.

CHAPTER NINETEEN

Recollections of you

The last night you held me close to your chest, I remember drifting into a peaceful slumber. That night I didn't have to dream of you (as it occurred), for one among many dreams of mine had come true. Each time you call me to see me, you could bet in certainty that I jump in joy like a happy kid exhilarated to go to the annual town fair. To me, your handsome childlike smile, and those welcoming eyes that twinkle, serve as worthwhile reasons for all the pep and high. I'd spend the preceding days looking for innumerable but effective ways by how I could make myself look like somebody who could hold your constant attention, and not let it deflect. I can't tell how I found myself soaked and drenched in your love, but however it is, I want you to know that you've meddled with my sanity. You have assumed all control of my senses, which once were mine. My heart no longer listens to what I have to say, all it does is nod and go scarlet whenever it sees you. Although I ask it to not let the spaces fill up any sooner, it willfully keeps on collecting hearts with your name written on them, in sheer non-compliance. There was a time when my face knew pretense, but as and when you came about, those unannounced smiles and bashful eyes scream of how you make me shrink with diffidence. Isn't it all very unjust that when you fall for someone, and want to make them yours in full measure, you can never affirm whether they too would fall for you? Why do I have to love someone who might never love me back? Why do I have to laugh, cry, blush, giggle, and do everything else because I'm knee deep into my emotions, without feeling clingy and descriptive of a woman who is obsessing over a man who might never be hers to call? Love amuses me with its constant tricks. The truth is, I never knew I'd smile for no reason just by looking at someone. I didn't know I'd build fairytales in my head just by being with someone. I never imagined I'd want someone to stay forever, each time they held my hand and brought it close to their face to kiss it. I seldom envisioned I'd want all my fantasies to come true with only one man. The more that I realize how unfair love and life is, the more I come to crave for your presence around me, and for you to hold me still through the storms.

Believe me when I say, the last time I mouthed my goodbye to you, my heart and mind had a sudden but inevitable fight. My mind told me I couldn't stay with you, for you had responsibilities and priorities that needed much more attention than me, while my heart wept in silence imagining the Christmas Eve without you. I know you aren't obligated to give me your time and focused attention, but truth is every morning I plead for constant conversations and surprise phone calls. Something about the idea of having you in my life, feels like the idea of mental tranquility taking over my mind and body. I could spend a thousand hours lying in silence yet in blissful moments, merely by resting my head against your chest. I could laugh and giggle all day, simply by watching you smile as you talk about your favorite cuisines, travel destinations, and the best of friends.

You had once taken a solemn promise from me, asking me to pledge for honesty and tell you whatever was contained in my heart, if it found a connection to you in any way. And it is today that I ask you, why haven't you fallen for me? Why didn't you ever feel the things that I have been feeling all the while? Why doesn't the silent nights, deep conversations, silly fights, long drives, similar playlists, love-making sessions, desire to be with each other, and the lasting hugs mean nothing to you? Am I yet a friend who's just good comfort to you, or do you see me as someone who could take good care of your precious heart someday? You see my love, it hurts to want to have you around me but not question your absence because we're still bound by the ring of uncertainty that speaks of possibilities rather than certainties.

I have wanted to tell you this since long enough now, and it's near time that you should know. The last time we were about to part, you sprayed your favorite fragrance on me, telling me (as I vividly recall), "you'd now smell of this for the next three days". One thing that you forgot to mention however was that, "You'd now smell of me, and it would remind you of my absence till the time I'm away". Ever since, my dear man, I have taken showers, and used a variety of gels and soaps, but the scent refuses to abandon my senses, and set me free. It's as if you've bound it by some spell that must torment me with your memories till the time I get to be held by you, again. Aren't you a sadist to watch me crumble every second as I crave your warm embrace, while you're roaming the big streets with your buddies and chomping down your favorite burritos without me?

I have laid my heart bare and exposed to you. Would you now take the reins of it in your hands, so it begins to feel alive again? It has pledged its loyalty to you, like a soldier vows for loyalty to his king. All it now awaits for is acceptance.

CHAPTER TWENTY

Patient love

They paint life into a mosaic of colors, both bright and somber. Describing the journey as maddening and exasperating, they still talk of a final destination that is wreathed in smiles. They say the sun sets every evening, but it rises yet again the next morning. And just like that, we must get on our feet and continue walking the road to the unknown, despite the countless times that we trip and fall. I had been walking along a similar path, regardless of the unannounced ordeals that awaited me. I wielded a shield of hope in hand, and possessed a terribly conflicted mind that clearly wasn't in sync with my soul's rhythm. Nevertheless, owing obedience and loyalty to my countable well wishers, I had to fathom the depth of my purpose, and the journey's end. But just as a lost traveler succumbs to the scorching heat of the nameless desert, after hours of wandering like a disoriented animal, separated from his herd, I too had found myself standing at a mountain high, from the top of which I could only see the glittering blue ocean. I too had reached an end, after walking clueless into the road less traveled. From the peak of the mountain, either of the two could be my possibility- I could choose to jump and drown myself in the surging waves as the heavy currents caught on to me, or I could let myself loose and swim through, till I found a shore to get back on.

It is times like these when you realize life often plays tricks on you. It is sudden moments like these that take you by sheer surprise, and when you feel like you've lost it all, a tiny ray of sunshine from somewhere far away tells you it was all a bad dream, and reality appears promising. Specific to me, the source of that glowing light was a young man in his late twenties, who simply stood by and let out an endearing smile that flooded my heart with overwhelming sweetness. He is a magician, oblivious of his supernatural powers that he possesses. He would smile at you, and all of the sudden you would feel your lips curve as your cheekbones gradually appear a tinge of berry, and just like that, you'll catch yourself smiling! His single touch could make your body tingle, as your heart would begin to beat ever so furiously, and your shortened breaths would remind you of the sudden jitter. He could take you into his arms and all that misery that had sworn it's loyalty to you, would abandon your soul in seconds, leaving you in tranquility and mental bliss. His voice isn't unusually coarse and dense, but his casual "hello" has the terrific ability to lift you up and get you dancing, each time you answer his call.

And just like that, he waved his magic wand and blinked his angelic eyes, and I knew even if I had nothing on the shore, I had to swim towards it. I knew drowning was not an option, since my journey hasn't yet concluded. Even though I might call him a savior, as he pulled me out of the tightening grip of damage and agony, he sternly asked me to become my own cure, for only I knew the bruises that were in need of remedy. Although I instantly gave him my timid heart, absolutely certain he would not toss it away; he took it but hadn't laid any claim yet. He kept it safe and still does, but has been careful to not wrap it up in promises that he can't keep. He requested for some good time, so he witnesses the growth of a strong woman in me, who would never shed a second tear but only laugh and live.

In my own world, I have made him mine, for I know he still is oblivious of the ascendency that he has on me. And although I plead my stars each night that someday he too makes me his, and kisses my hand to promise a lifetime of togetherness, I fear the Universe would help my cause, considering history and its games with me. Nevertheless a New Year has begun, and I no longer rely on the heavens for my rewards, but on my actions as testimony to why I deserve what I've been asking for. Somewhere deep within, I know I ain't a terrible human. Somehow I know I can love like no other. And some way I'm certain, only he can love me the right way. The only thing I await is for our stars to align.

And the day that happens, I'd finally be able to call myself an author of my own life, rather than a storyteller who creates lives. My fiction would someday turn authentic, and something tells me we're meant to be.

CHAPTER TWENTY-ONE

Wistful Longings

Last evening while I was on my way back from an exhausting yet eventful day, I watched the reddish, gleaming sun gently camouflage itself with the hovering grayish clouds, as the towering trees quickly moved past my sight, with the eventually speeding car. I gazed at the ginger hued sky, and reminisced about you, like an adolescent gets nostalgic about his old days, while passing by the local fair. It's funny how you only reckon the value of the moments spent, when the present becomes the past, and all you could do is rewind back.

I looked towards the passenger seat, and pictured myself there, staring outside the car window, and asking you to change the music, as you casually drive through the wilderness that leads to the highway. As you'd do the needful, I'd deliberately mouth the lyrics (as if dedicating the entire art to you) and lean on your shoulder, as I slowly place my palm on yours, and you eventually tighten your grip.

It's not so cold in here, seems like winter has offered mercy to my townspeople. And so, I'm compelled to wander back to that night in December, when the morning fog was enough to envelop the entire atmosphere in a blanket of mist and haze, as the two of us sat with gritted teeth and icy cold hands, struggling to keep up against the dropping temperature. I remember how you told me about the airplane that had just taken off from quite a distance, but how the sound was still clear enough for us to think it was closer. Just a while later, we walked hand in hand, back to the room, somewhat satisfied that we lived one of the fantasies that romance novels often talk of. By five in the morning, I watched you drift to a deep slumber, right in my arms.

Whenever I watch the streets get cluttered with people, I cannot help but think of how you'd pull me out of the crowd, holding my hand, like you did on that Christmas Eve, as I watched you become protective for me. No wonder comfort is inevitable when you're around, regardless of however chaotic the surrounding gets.

There is something unusually pleasing about those unexpected calls that come to me. Although at most times, the conversation doesn't really last long because one of us has to leave, the realization that you thought of me, overwhelms me with a surging sense of pride. Unknowingly, I look myself in the mirror and catch myself grinning, as the people around me eye me with suspicion. Little do they know that sometimes, happiness can just mean a person and his thoughts, and not just moments.

I'll tell you a very weird thing that has irked my conscience last night. The fact that you're home yet you don't feel like it; makes you wonder if home is truly where the heart is. And although a part of me still exists in here, a significant chunk was what I had handed you over. And now, wherever I go, I look for my home, and probably you're just it.

It's ironic to see how fondness can build with someone you've not been friends with since you were six, or even with someone you never vaguely imagined to come across. It's just a sudden, unplanned encounter, and inevitable conversations lead to tiny moments of togetherness, and in a blink of an eye, you reckon how similar you both are. And just like that, memories wield enough power to fill up space inside you, and with time you realize it's something special- so much special that an eternity of togetherness might be all that you're looking for.

The afternoon I had boarded my flight and was all set to fly back home, I felt a sharp pain in me as I watched the aircraft gradually head for takeoff. While some passengers were thrilled to fly back to their families, yet others were either traveling for work or something specific. I however, felt like I was flying away from my family. Although a family comprises of more than one person, I knew to me you were everything, for the flooding tears in my eyes testified the reckoning. If miracles were real, I would've run back to you that afternoon, only to never leave.

Like you said to me the night before, "slow and steady lasts longer". So if you ask for even a year, only to fully love me as who I am, I give to you all of it, as we both want it to last an eternity- an eternity that watches us grow from young lovers, to potential partners who would continue to hold on even when the Universe falls apart.

I can't tell if you miss me the way you describe you do. But rest assured, I'd tell you forgetting me isn't easy, for our hearts are intertwined and our fate has been decided. We'd walk through it together; the day you know it's time.

CHAPTER TWENTY-TWO

Dear love,

To my dear love,

It's been weeks since I've fallen for your noble heart, and my string of thoughts have been pirouetting since, around the moments that I wish to spend with you. Just the other night, I picked up my quill (that grandpa had left me, from this little antiquated box of treasured items) and dipped it in the brimming bottle of ink, as I knew I'd have pages to fill. I'd have written it all in a long, never ending letter containing all my emotions that make me long for your presence, and sent you through that old postman riding his bicycle, all the way to your little, happy abode. However, what if it found its way to your mother, and somehow she went through the contents of it? She'd learn of a young woman deeply missed by her son, and adored equally so, but yet not his lover neither his lady luck. What would you have said to her, if she chose to ask you about my place in your golden and inimitable heart? Would you tell her I'm just a friend whose company amuses you, so much so that you've touched her in ways in which a man touches his beloved, or would you tell her you've given me my heart, and have been waiting to confess your love for me? Don't you worry, for I've spared you the horror. Only so you do not have to frame the sentences which your heart doesn't wish for you to, I'm typing down every emotion, every desire, and every sentiment with the same fervor, only so you're not bereft of the passion that consumes me.

When at the break of dawn, as the rays of the sun stealthily peek through the translucent night sky, I want to find myself laying beside you as you turn to your right, deeply asleep.

I wish to be the face you wake up to see in the middle of the night, after a rough day at work, when a sudden nightmare torments you.

When you long for peace after the arduous weekdays come to a close, I want to be your safe haven in whose embrace you feel at harmony and solitude.

I want to sing to you on days that don't look as good, in my not-so-sweet but childlike voice, as you rest your head on my thighs, and I run my fingers through your long, messy hair, scoffing at you in sarcasm for yet not chopping them off.

I want to make you your California burritos and that unknown dish you yet don't seem to recall, when you find yourself running out of money. I'd plan a sweet, little date with home-cooked food, two cans of ginger ale, and your comfort French fries, feasting while grooving to your classic electronic playlists, pointing out the sudden but smooth transitions together as and when they occurred.

I want to laugh with your mother at your protruding tummy, as you complain about the lack of time for gym sessions due to piling work load. And when alone, I'd run my hands on it and smirk at you, while I'd still call you steaming hot and feisty.

I want to hop in your car at the graveyard hour, as you turn on the heater, and simply sit and talk about science, comets, stars, and the night sky, and lean in to kiss your forehead each time you say, "I'm clearly a boring person to be with".

I want us to drive without a destination, and suddenly stop in the middle of a deserted highway, as you put on the shades and come closer to me, wanting to make me all yours. I'd still go crimson, for I adore you beyond measure, but I'm certain I'd let go when your actions would summon my senses.

I want to fight with you like a teenage kid, but I'd want you to come to me after it all. Even if you don't, I can picture myself walking timidly towards you, for I'd not be able to spend minutes not talking to you.

I want us to tour the world in the craziest outfits that you decide for me, and kiss under the lamppost, or hug in front of the sea, as the world watches us being deeply engrossed in each other.

I'd slowly kiss your neck as I breathe on it while you attend meetings with those international chicks, as you fumble for words, and mix up your figures and statistics. But something tells me you'd not rebuke me still, rather punish me with kisses.

We'd clean up our little house, and build ourselves a cozy place, where we'd sit and talk about our dreams, and desires, and discuss the names of our kids, laughing at our own suggestions.

We'd dance around the fireplace every Christmas, and cling our empty glasses (I know you'd not drink wine either) on every New Year's Eve and look at each other smiling, recalling how we no longer need a 'night stay' for we're now living together.

I want us to turn eighty, struggling to stand still with our canes in hand, as I bake you cookies and you tell me I look beautiful, as my hair turns grey and my skin catches wrinkles, and my breasts begin to sag.

I want us to do gardening on Sundays, go cycling on Saturdays, spend surprise dates once a weekday, finish a movie every Friday, visit our parents every two weeks, call friends once a month, have a barbeque with the cousins, share bedtime stories with our children, make love like college lovers, go for prayers together, have fun at the local grocery store as I plead you for ramen and you tell me you don't like them, try out hobbies together, and do every little thing with you that you've only imagined of doing.

Isn't it surprising how love already makes you imagine a zillion things, as you get all jittery and begin to work for the future that you wish to share with your lover? Love surely is a happy thing, only if the souls vouch for permanency and strength, even when the world decides to cave in on you.

If I get to have just one chance at complete honesty, would you please tell me if you ever feel a thing for me? Would you please not let me build my castles if you've chosen to not reside in them? Would you please tell me if you're not in love, for it hurts to not be loved back? Would you stay as my dream boy but walk me out for another man to claim me? Oh dear love, I'd crumble into bits as I'd watch you abandon my hand and walk away into the brighter side, for my love for you has grown deeper, and I want you to make me yours forever. So tell me then, would you love me forever?

Reckonings Of The Past

I was perhaps delusional in thinking I found the man I had been praying for, the day our paths crossed and our eyes met. None but my imbecile heart is to be blamed, for believing love was an easy game. It has now occurred to me that rationality surrenders itself to spontaneous but nonsensical decisions, when the soul is in a debilitated state, and is now sapped by the constant downturn of events. You were just another human, and I was a deluded lover. The tiniest things that were expected of a nice man, made me rejoice in bliss when you exposed me to them. I laugh at the darkened irony as I realize the merest form of affection seemed like an unmatched show of love to me, as I eventually placed you on the pedestal, burdening you with constant praises and frequent acknowledgement, when none of it had been necessary. If at all anything, it fooled you into believing my life was in your hands, and the day you decide to withhold the reins, I'd succumb to death and misery. Little did you realize I was just a lover you had never come across, the kind that possessed overwhelming loyalty and never accepted bowing down to inevitable friction and war of words. You were just a novice, who wasn't capable of handling love that you only read about in books and poetry. You had been a child who struggled to maintain balance between competing preferences. Although I stood by firm, assuring you each time that I'd help you sail through it all, your wicked mind had already been consumed with a heightened sense of self-esteem. You chose to give up on companionship, rather than reflecting on your downsides. You chose to abandon the intense intimacy that we shared, rather than attempting to settle your conflicted brain. And just like an equally foolish and dim-witted romantic, I made you the muse of all my art. I would scribble on countless pages, expressing my overwhelming grief and crumbling emotions through fine words of fancy literature, and watched the world call it aesthetic. While the readers found creativity, sheer witnesses spotted the concealed bruises that would occasionally show up. You made me into a writer of life, whose experiences served as significant lessons for young boys and girls who misjudged infatuation.

What's even more surprising however, is how you had begun with a saintly smile and a heart of gold. You denied me a chance to question sudden spurts of blissful romance. You'd do everything necessary to confirm my presence in your dull and somber life. You wanted my body, for you had never devoured one before, and I offered it to you bereft of every hesitation. You doubted my devotion, and I surpassed every barrier to prove to you the depths of my fondness for you. I was duped into thinking you resemble a handsome God; while it is now that I reckon how I was unaware of what an average looked like. You demanded enough space, and asked for time, and like an obedient kid, I nodded to it all. You disappeared in the day, and I kept my calm, giving reassurances to myself that it's all just a phase. When at night you'd return to me, asking me to quench your lust, I'd do all you'd ask for, in the name of love that never existed. I had been deceived all the while, handing you over tons of acceptance, attention, concern, and attachment; while you tossed them all away into the dumpster you had kept safe for me. I thought it was love, while in reality it was my lovesick but traumatized heart that did not want to experience damage by accepting the truth that existed.

But don't you worry, dear silly child, for we have concluded our bond. I understand you aren't yet grown enough to attain a deeper perspective. I however need you to know that I still have unheard and unseen stories to look for, and without you by my side, I'm certain I'd be fortunate. Two months after deeply scrutinizing and comprehending your hoax that you very confidently termed as 'love', I met a man who seems built by the tragedies of life, so much so that his powerful words have transformed an entire year for me. Although our emotions have been spoken of, and we sense an intimacy as we stare into each other's eyes, we're yet to commit to love as by now I've learnt to experience before inferring. So if you had been my muse, and if the pain that you gave me molded me into a heartbroken poet, this man's actions have turned me into a sensible young woman fuelled with insights. I hope with time, your mind grows and your heart becomes accepting, and someday you realize you weren't ever the God that others joked about to you.

• 67 •

My Own Reflections

In my twenty-two years of existing as a somewhat traumatized, socially anxious, reticent, and timid adult woman, who has had her fair share of highs and lows in life, I have considered myself fortunate enough to have lived through an incredible amount of significant experiences that have had a crucial role to play in my understanding of relationships. Over the years I have grown up to become a person who acknowledges and fully accepts the idea that the 'maturity' of an individual is what can be gauged through his/her experiences and struggles that they had to endure, throughout their lives. A teenage boy, who has grown up as an abandoned kid in the nearby orphanage, would know about the grief of desertion better than an adolescent who has grown up under the care of overwhelmingly preoccupied guardians. Similarly, an adolescent who has seen dozens of relationships build and break would know about the trauma of heartbreak in a better way, than a naïve young girl in her twenties who is reeling from the culmination of a month-old bond.

One recurring thought that has kept my conscience preoccupied for months now, has been the persistent question of why has pain become an inalienable part of every relationship, so much so that it never subsides but only grows in intensity. I have heard women complain of how they have continued to pour in all their love, by planning out sudden surprises, designing special cakes, doodling cute gift cards, and even taking care of every little activity, and yet get no such gesture as a means of reciprocation. They comprehend it as a 'lack of effort'. On the other hand, I also hear men talking about how they are never understood in ways that they ought to be, which ultimately builds the foundation for an inevitable split as a consequence of eminent conflict. Gradually the process of healing that follows is accompanied by isolation to a point where you begin feeling no one is compatible enough for you. All of it makes me wonder if ending an age-old bond of love has become that easy of a task. Whom do we blame for this unfortunate end, is it the overly loving women who are way too emotionally vulnerable and weak at heart, or is it the emotionally restricted, toughened, and aggressive men who feel forced to strictly adhere to the supposed idea of masculinity?

This is exactly where there develops an urgent need to take into account the societal differences between the two genders. Books have contributed significantly to our understanding of women and how they perform their roles in society, as also how their entire orientation appears to be. Ironically, however, there is little or no discussion around the psychology of men, who are generally and simplistically described as those who need to work to feed a family. We do not know how a man's brain works when he falls in love, or what his brain does when he feels pain and agony. I assume a better understanding of the 'male psychology' would help us look into how their 'lack of effort' unknowingly leads to the end of year-long chapters of love and romance. Since women feel too much, it wouldn't be wrong to suggest that things don't end up on the same page since men feel so little. What one might view as a lack of maturity might in reality be his lack of emotional availability since he is already too cluttered in his head. Therefore it might be wrong to label him as a faulty lover when in actuality he is just a naïve boy who is yet to grow up into a man, who finally has all means to devote equal time to his partner and his goals. Growing up is a steady process, and we simply cannot expect someone to step into the shoes of a man in his late thirties one morning, who has all his priorities sorted and settled.

As surprising as it may sound, studies suggest that men desire more or less the same things that a woman desires from a relationship. Some of these desires stem from the need to feel a deeper sense of connection, effective means of communication, and wanting to be felt and heard, to be listened to. If we go by the general idea that suggests 'women are the most complicated beings to be comprehended fully', the scientific data clears up some air and puts forth the conclusion that men and women are more alike than significantly different when it comes down to their needs and mental orientation. However, one interesting point of difference could be indicative of the fact that men feel the strict need to adhere to the norms of masculinity, which in a way leads them to suppress the emotions necessary for any intimate relationship. The general way in which men are dismissed as 'genetically deficient' beings when it comes to their inability to express themselves entirely, or talk about their innermost troubles openly, makes them avoid communication that is way too intimate and deep. To comprehend this situation, it may be necessary for us to look into how boys are conditioned in their societies since their childhood, and how such conditioning shapes their minds in a way that they grow up to be unable to handle conflict in a relationship. No wonder, this is why we say women tend to be ahead of the curve when it comes to maturity as compared to that of men. This is probably because as women, we are taught to be accountable and responsible for our actions, be emotionally available, excel in child care, and be the submissive self who is always soft-hearted and benevolent. Unlike these women, men are simply made familiar with the idea that someday they would have to hold a job well enough to sustain their families and become the protective guard that can never break even in times of adversity. The emphasis on building them as such rigid personalities becomes so high that they are seldom told to share their fears or emotions, express hurt, or vent it out. Rather, anger develops as a defense mechanism through which they display their weakest versions through violent actions, deluded by the idea that it makes them appear strong. The constant need to not express any pain, even when they feel it in extremes, builds up their ego which becomes way too adamant to ever accept defeat.

Beginning in boyhood, men are expected to try and conform to the societal norms of masculinity. Consequentially therefore, men grow up to control their innermost emotions and make sure to not appear 'vulnerable' at any cost. Failure is sinister to them, as society enforces upon them the need to build and feed a family, so much so that a man staying at home and looking after the kids appears to be an idealistic situation. To them, earning enough is not just a testimony to their ability to feed a family but also the point of validation that they can now be viewed as a potential life partner. Therefore the pressure to build a stable future is such that the constant frightening concern alienates them from the reality. The perturbing thought of coming at par with his social circle who already have the biggest positions in reputed companies, the upcoming shame from the society, family, and partner in case of failure at work, the inevitable frustration due to not being able to open up about the deepest emotions, and the overpowering burden of looking after his family and taking control of all responsibilities, can break a man so much so that he barely finds any time to reflect at himself, rather than focusing on how he could contribute to a healthy love life. Different men have different ways and strategies to cope up with such a depressing and demanding phase. Some move out of their shells and decide to communicate, irrespective of the outcomes. Some find solace in distancing themselves from the world, and hustling in silence. Some turn to alcohol, misinterpreting it as an effective solution to all their misery.

This is however not to suggest that 'benevolent sexism' or attributing maturity to a specific gender is the best thing to do. Describing boys as immature and girls as mature may lead women to accept the indecent and inappropriate behaviors of men, with the perception that 'men will be men'. Likewise, men would never learn to take responsibility for their actions, and rather would justify themselves as "this is how I am".

Therefore in every romantic relationship, the conflicted psyche of men and the aspect of benevolent sexism, that works in continuing the inevitable conflict eventually drains the bond of love and mutual understanding. While women do every possible thing to keep the spark going and alive, men's inability to stay consistent eventually washes away all efforts. In this evident conundrum, none is to be blamed for their individual troubles, but the solution lies in mutual cooperation. If the love for the significant other has made you fall to your knees, move beyond your boundaries, embrace change, experience intimacy, visualize a happy future infused with success and excitement, and has made you dance with joy, then that same love is worth saving.

Underneath the differential conditioning of the two genders, there is a child who desires love, and wishes someone to be okay with them when they aren't winning. Men want women to talk to them about their day (just like women want the same for themselves). Men utterly despise the idea of dependency when it comes to emotional support. This is because such a form of dependency would make him feel the burden of constantly presenting himself as your next 'boost' rather than his authentic self. In such a situation, women would be more susceptible to criticizing their partners. The solution therefore lies in accepting yourself and embracing self-love.

In fear of stigmatization, most men tend to avoid communicating their vulnerable thoughts. Hence, if a man speaks about his insecurities, he needs to be taken seriously and questioned for his concerns, so much so that he feels the joy of effective communication, and the level of intimacy further enhances. A man would love to be viewed as a real person who is (for a moment) free of control and agendas for the day. Deep down therefore, the wants and desires of both the partners in every relationship are way too similar. The problem lies in believing that support is demanded by only either of them. The social requirement of men to work as emotionally reliant beings often makes them unable to speak about their needs from a relationship. They constantly 'supervise' the signs of potential conflict in their partners, the result of which leads them to blame themselves for their failure. Over time, the extent of them avoiding conflict becomes so much that eventually they cede from trying. It is necessary for us women to realize that men value independence more than intimacy. And therefore the constant need for time and space is necessary to let them breathe and not feel suffocated by any bond. Men demand security and certainty just as we do, and that comes from approval of him and his goals. Trust builds up security, and that alone is enough to overcome the worst of hurdles.

To put it simply, for a relationship to work, we want the boys to become better men for us. And that can only be done if we consider them similar to us, and in need of the same reassurances that we yearn for. If love is to stay, the two individuals have to know that it's only supposed to get better. The 'efforts' start from trying to gauge what's going on inside, rather than imposing labels that categorize them as 'immature', 'toxic', or 'cheats', and this goes both ways.

DIFFICULT CONVERSATIONS

THE RIGHT WAY

2 Manuscripts in 1 Book, Including: How to Talk to People and How to Ask Questions

Dean Mack

More by Dean Mack

Discover all books from the Social Skills Best Seller Series by Dean Mack at:

bit.ly/dean-mack

Book 1: *How to Flirt*

Book 2: *How to Start a Conversation*

Book 3: *How to Talk to People*

Book 4: *How to Ask Questions*

Book 5: *How to Be Funny*

Book 6: *How to Influence People*

Book 7: *How to Attract Men*

Book 8: *How to Attract Women*

Themed book bundles available at discounted prices:

bit.ly/dean-mack